Contents

Photography: Betsy Baker, 56, 57, 64. Glenn Burkland, 26, 27, 91. Michael Gilroy, 10, 30, 31, 79. Ray Hanson, 6, 70, bottom. Harry V. Lacey, title page, 49, 85. A. J. Mobbs, 74. Mervin F. Roberts, 7, 11, 14, 15, 18, 19, 23, 33, 66, 67, 70, top, 75, 78, 82, 83, 86, 87. Vincent Serbin, 32. Matthew M. Vriends, endpapers, 71. Courtesy of Vogelpark Walsrode, 90.

ISBN 0-87666-812-0

Distributed in the UNITED STATES by T.F.H. Publications, Inc., 211 West Sylvania Avenue, Neptune City, NJ 07753; in CANADA by H & L Pet Supplies Inc., 27 Kingston Crescent, Kitchener, Ontario N2B 2T6; Rolf C. Hagen Ltd., 3225 Sartelon Street, Montreal 382 Quebec; in ENGLAND by T.F.H. Publications Limited, 4 Kier Park, Ascot, Berkshire SL5 7DS; in AUSTRALIA AND THE SOUTH PACIFIC by T.F.H. (Australia) Pty. Ltd., Box 149, Brookvale 2100 N.S.W., Australia; in NEW ZEALAND by Ross Haines & Son, Ltd., 18 Monmouth Street, Grey Lynn, Auckland 2 New Zealand; in SINGAPORE AND MALAYSIA by MPH Distributors Pte., 71-77 Stamford Road, Singapore 0617; in the PHILIPPINES by Bio-Research, 5 Lippay Street, San Lorenzo Village, Makati, Rizal; in SOUTH AFRICA by Multipet Pty. Ltd., 30 Turners Avenue, Durban 4001. Published by T.F.H. Publications Inc., Ltd., the British Crown Colony of Hong Kong.

GOULDIAN FINCHES

Mervin F. Roberts

Left and below: A Red-headed male. Both Black- and Red-headedness are sex-linked traits. Select a healthy bird like this one (*below*), one that holds its feathers closely, has bright eyes, and perches without squatting.

The Gouldian Finch

"Oh, that bird is so beautiful! What is it called? It must be very tropical, very delicate, and very expensive—is it? Do I dare to own one or two?" These questions are always the same, and they often come so fast that I cannot articulate the answers until the inquirer pauses for a breath. Then I say, "One, Gouldian Finch; two, yes; three, yes." But the inquirer has already forgotten the questions, so here is a book about the Gouldian Finch: a reasonable challenge with a tremendous reward.

The whole bird is only five to five-and-a-half inches long, from the tip of its bill to the pointed ends of its two long central tail feathers, and by weight it costs only a little less than the price of gold. Still, breeders cannot keep up with the demand.

Since this book contains unretouched natural color photographs, no written color descriptions are necessary. The intention here is to help you to select, feed, cage, and care for all Gouldian Finches, regardless of their color.

CLASSIFICATION

Classification is a fancy word for locating an organism in the chart or table commonly called the Tree of Life. Of course, since it was developed by humans, it puts you and me at the top of the heap. If you are not familiar with the classification process, it seems absurdly simple; but, like most things in nature, it is not. We can be grateful that at least the first few major points are easy. The finer points have driven great minds to the bottle, or worse. So, for what it's worth, here is the Gouldian Finch in the Tree of Life.

Kingdom: ANIMALIA. Animal, as opposed to vegetable or fungus.

Phylum: CHORDATA. Animals whose central nervous systems are dorsally situated. By this definition, we have now excluded mollusks, insects, worms, and of course all single-celled organisms.

Subphylum: VERTEBRATA. Cartilage or bone encloses at least part of the central nervous system. Some classifiers make this a phylum. Some classifiers add Craniata, for those animals who have the head end of their central nervous system enclosed in a cranium, or skull.

Class: AVES. The birds, warm-blooded, egg-laying, feathered vertebrates. There are about 9,000 species within 28 or so orders.

Order: PASSERIFORMES. Birds that perch and sing. They have four toes on each foot. The toes are joined at the same level, and three of them point forward. By contrast, owls and parrots have two toes forward and two aft on each foot. There are no webs between the toes; ducks, gulls, geese and swans exit here. Young are nidicolous; that is, they are hatched naked, blind, and helpless, which eliminates poultry and rails. Generally, parent birds take care of their young, but a few species are brood parasites. There are, in this order, about 75 families containing about 5,100 species.

Family: ESTRILDIDAE. Commonly called estrildid finches, or waxbills. Here we also find the grassfinches and mannikins. Their nestlings have decorated palates and tongues; they beg for food by crouching and twisting their necks (with their mouths opened wide) and waving their heads. Estrildids mature rapidly, often in only a few months. According to some authorities, there are 107 or so species in this family, including Zebra Finches and Java Sparrows.

Genus: In 1844 John Gould called it *Amadina*. In 1862 Reichenbach said this genus should be called *Chloebia*. In 1943 Jean Delacour placed it in the genus *Poephila*. In 1962 and 1967 Klaus Immelmann suggested that until more information is accumulated and interpreted we had best "place the genus for itself. In this case *Chloebia* Reichenbach 1862 is the oldest name available." Dr. Immelmann goes on to suggest that "the Gouldian Finch may represent a link between *Lonchura* and *Erythrura*." In 1975 Cyril Rogers said *Erythrura*.

Species: GOULDIAE. Named by John Gould in 1844 in honor of his wife, who accompanied him in his Australian explorations.

So here we have a bird whose specific name is universally accepted but whose generic name is cloudy. Don't let it trouble you. Over the course of years, this bird has also been called the Purple-breasted Finch, the Painted Finch, and the Rainbow Finch, but none of these names should be used anymore. *Emblema picta* has long been known as the Painted Finch. The other names, Rainbow Finch and Purple-breasted Finch, are not in common use anywhere. The Germans and Dutch call it the *Gouldamadine,* and the French commonly refer to it as the *Diamant de Gould*.

Let us call it the Gouldian Finch, and everyone will know precisely what we are referring to. No other bird in the world resembles it.

I suggest that if you must be "scientific," you would be well advised to call it *Chloebia gouldiae* (Gould) 1844 and, again, any knowledgeable aviculturist will know what you are referring to.

As I mentioned before, the first written description of this bird was by John Gould, and the record in formal terms is *Amadina gouldiae* in *Birds Austr.,*pt. 15 (vol. III, pl. 88), 1 June 1844; Victoria River, Northern Territory.

Gould accomplished an unusual thing with this bird in terms of zoological nomenclature. He himself got the name of the bird to resemble his own name. In the system established a hundred years previously by Linnaeus (kingdom, phylum, class, etc.), living forms are named by the person who first publishes their description. By con-

A pair of young Red-headed hens (*above*). Often head feathers are molted simultaneously so that the entire head is covered with sheaths. A pair of Red-headed adults (*facing page*). The hen's bill has darkened, indicating that she has come into breeding condition.

vention a describer does not name the organism after himself. Now what John Gould did in 1844 was to discover, describe, and name the species in honor of a Gould who happened to be his own wife, Mrs. John Gould. This is why the ending of the word is -ae. This is the Latin designator for female. I must admit that I do not know if Mrs. Gould's maiden name was by coincidence also Gould.

The Gouldian Finch has been hybridized only once, and in that instance it was a male Gouldian mated with a female Blue-faced Parrot-Finch. The offspring died leaving no progeny.

GOULDIANS IN THE WILD

From its brilliant and diverse colors you correctly surmise that the Gouldian Finch is a tropical bird. It is found only in northern (tropical) Australia and only as far south on that island continent as the 19th parallel of latitude. Americans should remember that Miami, Florida is about 26 degrees of latitude from the equator. A Gouldian, then, is truly a tropical bird. Pet keepers everywhere should remind themselves that they cannot remake the Gouldian Finch to suit their climate. Even a few days of 50 F. (10 C.) is too cold for too long.

From the shape of its bill you correctly surmise that this bird is an eater of small grass seeds. It picks them up, one at a time, and (unlike a pigeon) it hulls them before swallowing the kernels. Although it isn't evident from their appearance, Gouldians in their native habitat are also highly insectivorous, especially during their breeding season. Field reports have them eating large quantities of flying termites, a high-protein animal food. This will be a challenge to you as an aviculturist, since flying termites aren't readily available to most bird keepers. After you find those termites, you will probably discover that your birds won't touch them. Most domestic Gouldian Finches are totally vegetarian. You may even have to employ another bird to teach them to eat hard-boiled egg.

Gouldians build sloppy nests, or, even more commonly, they nest in a hollow limb or a hollow tree. Frequently the five-to-seven relatively large, creamy white eggs are laid right on the soft, punky wood in such a hollow. The white eggs suggest a dark nest cavity—woodpecker eggs are also white, but, by contrast, robin eggs, in open nests, are blue. As a matter of fact, most Gouldian nests are dark inside.

This leads to an interesting phenomenon: the sides of the mouth of every baby Gouldian Finch have brilliant, turquoise-colored luminous spots which probably guide the parents when they come with food. The luminous marks shrink and disappear once the babies leave their nest. Although each species of Australian finch has its own distinctive pattern of mouth markings, these marks have no material effect on the birds which are propagated in cages. This is proven by the fact that Gouldians can be fostered by other species whose nestlings have different patterns.

The bill color of adult males in breeding condition is ivory- or beige-pink with a rosy tip. Females in breeding condition have dark gray (slate) bills, as do the juveniles until they have molted. Females out of breeding condition have lighter-colored bills. One exception is the yellow-headed, or yellow-faced, form, in which the bill is tinged with yellow rather than pink.

Wild Gouldian Finches exhibit three color phases: black-faced, red-faced, and yellow-faced. These strains are established in captivity, and, much like neckties, you pay your money and you take your choice. Some bird keepers say black or red or yellow "-headed" and others say "faced." They are all talking about the same birds. Among captive Gouldians, several color mutations have occurred. There have been albino, lutino, pied, white-breasted, and blue-breasted varieties. The colors of juveniles and females are more subdued than those of males.

Select a Gould that is in full adult plumage, like the Red-headed female left, to be certain of its head color. The juvenile below will retain its drab green and gray coloring until its first molt, at which time head color and sex can be determined.

Selecting and Housing Gouldians

CHOOSING A BIRD

If you have room in your flight for one or two additional nonaggressive finches, and the temperature in your bird room averages 75 F. but never goes below 50 F., then you are ready to acquire Gouldians. Go at it slowly and carefully. Select a good-looking bird with smooth, tight feathers, plenty of flesh on its breast, bright eyes, and erect carriage. Don't choose a snoozer or a sloucher or a blinker or a puffer or a wet-bottomed bird.

Try to obtain a specimen which is in full adult plumage. If you choose a juvenile, you will not know whether its face will be red or black. You won't even be able to determine its sex. If you want the most color and can afford only one bird, get an adult male. Females are certainly beautiful, but males are even more beautiful. Be prepared to pay a big premium for blue-breasted or white-breasted birds. Don't buy a bird which you cannot afford to lose.

Juveniles are most vulnerable to loss until they complete

their first molt. This may take place anytime between four and eighteen months of age, depending on temperature and food supply. Remember that we have taken these birds from the tropical areas of Australia where they eat not only seeds but also termites. They have come a long way in a short time.

All the tail feathers in juveniles of both sexes are rounded, so don't choose a bird whose tail has no long, pointed central feathers—this is a sure sign that the juvenile molt has not ended.

TAMING AND TRAINING

Tame?—yes! Train?—no! If you use the crow or one of the popular parrots as a standard, then a Gouldian rates fairly low. Birds that are hand-reared are often the most easily tamed and trained. The finch, being tiny at birth, is very hard to hand-feed, especially since the seeds it eats must be hulled. By contrast, you can easily hand-rear a very young crow on hamburger, berries, green peas, and corn, and it will thrive.

If you keep your Gouldians in cages and visit them daily, they will become fearlessly tame; you will find that even the vacuum cleaner will not upset them. Yes, they are easily tamed, but don't expect one of these birds to spend hours on your shoulder whispering sweet nothings in your ear—it's the wrong bird for that.

Gouldians are not smart like talking parrots or trained falcons or racing pigeons or geese, but they do respond to new situations with more than random flutterings, meaningless chirps and leaps, or short flights from one perch to another. Move any article in the cage or aviary, and every bird will be on it, in it, over it within minutes. A new nest box or a handful of dry grass or a clump of sod or even a piece of fresh cuttlebone will get close, one-eyed scrutiny from every healthy Gouldian Finch. They are very inquisitive.

HOUSING

If you plan on an outdoor, ground-level aviary, wonderful! Gouldians do well in them, especially if they are planted with tough plants. A tender leaf will end up on the floor. Be sure you have buried galvanized wire mesh deep-

An illustration of an outdoor aviary, which provides bathing and drinking water, lots of natural perches, plenty of room for free flight, and an entrance into an indoor flight during inclement weather.

ly in the ground so as to keep out rats, mice, weasels, cats, and other vermin and predators.

The ideal wire mesh is three-eighths-inch square, or three-eighths by one inch. Most adult Gouldian Finches will not get through a one-half by one-inch opening, but juveniles might and some of the smaller finches you may also acquire might—and young mice can certainly get through one-half by one, perhaps even one-half square. Three-eighths-inch-square mesh seems to keep all birds in and all mammals out.

Incidentally, mice are not predators. They don't bite the birds, but nevertheless they can cause the birds to die. Mice are nocturnal, and Gouldian Finches are diurnal, so the birds (which are caged and unable to get away) will be kept awake until they waste away from lack of sleep. Mice also foul the birds' food.

The cage or aviary for your finches should have provision for food, drinking water, bathing water, grit, perching, nesting (if this is what you have in mind), and a place to hang a cuttlebone—not too difficult or costly when you consider the pleasure these birds will provide.

Some Gouldian Finches seem perfectly happy to perch on branches that are small in diameter relative to the size of their feet; however, it is best to provide perches with a variety of thicknesses to help the birds exercise their feet and legs. The outside flight (*facing page*) of the author's aviary. The finches kept here can perch outside in the fresh air and sunshine or retreat inside through the windows.

You should furnish perches of various diameters and shapes. Grasping a variety of shapes and sizes makes for good muscle tone. Also, do *not* use perches with sand, sandpaper, or abrasives on them for purposes of keeping your birds' claws in good condition; instead, check your birds and, if necessary, clip their claws just long enough to miss the blood vessel. In some situations birds will go for years without needing a claw clipping.

If you install potted plants, the birds will certainly spend a lot of time perching, picking, and climbing. You should aim at something tough and not poisonous. A fruit tree or a privet or a forsythia or a honeysuckle bush might be good to try. Red and white cedars are always green, but a bit coarse. One four-foot cedar tree in the author's aviary was an especially popular perching place, and the birds never ever picked at the foliage. Don't spend a lot of money on the tree, and don't waste effort on something which is in flower—you may discover that your birds prefer to have the petals on the floor, and they surely will accomplish their version of interior decoration in spite of your best-laid plans.

Zebra Finches and Society Finches tolerate wide variation in humidity, to a point where you can assume that if you can stand it, so can they. This is not the case for Gouldians. They are accustomed to higher humidity than is found in most American homes. Thus, they do well in a greenhouse. If you maintain an aviary, stock it with numerous, well-watered plants. If you have a bird room, mist it frequently or maintain an aquarium nearby. If you cage your birds in a multiple-use room, at least offer your birds a fresh bath every day. The ideal humidity for a temperature of 68 F. (20 C.) is 60%. For 75 F. (24 C.) the relative humidity should be closer to 70%.

Novice bird keepers are prone to let their enthusiasm overpower good judgment in determining how many birds to keep in one cage or aviary. Overstocking is absurd, especially for a beginner. It can only lead to disaster through disease, incompatibility, bullying, parasite problems, or worse.

Buy the largest cage or build the largest aviary you can afford, and then start with the smallest number of birds you can imagine for the space. Try this cage formula: the first cubic foot is to be vacant, then for each Gouldian Finch you should provide at least one additional cubic foot. A cage of two cubic feet is right for one bird; three cubic feet will accommodate two birds. Breeding cages should be even larger. Aviaries for Gouldians should provide even more space per bird, since most aviaries are less efficient when it comes to perches and private areas. By the time you know enough about this species to crowd them, you will no longer need the advice in this book—but my suggestion is that you make haste slowly.

GOULDIANS WITH OTHER BIRDS

An aviary or a large cage with several species of finches is certainly attractive, and for many bird keepers, Gouldians are the prize jewels. But with jewels you must observe some precautions. First, don't crowd your birds. Some pet shops may display more birds in each cage than they should. They have a labor cost and a real-estate problem which do not obtain in your home. It is hard to make an inflexible rule, but for each pair of birds, in mixed company especially, there should be at least a couple of cubic feet of cage space. A pair of Gouldians usually do get along with each other, but they don't get cozy with each other—or with other species, for that matter. For starters, provide a perch for each bird in the cage. If the cage becomes so full of perches that the birds cannot fly, you will know you have gone too far.

Now as to which birds to mix with Gouldians, I again suggest you go very slowly. Society Finches and Zebras are so social and nosy that I believe they actually annoy Gouldians, especially if any of the various birds pair up and try to breed. Try Lavenders, Red-ears, Bichenos, cordonbleus and other small seedeating finches. Although the Gouldian is larger than a Zebra Finch, a pair of Zebras will easily dominate a cage full of Gouldians. Really now, when you crowd your birds, what are you trying to accomplish?

SECURITY

There are several aspects to this section. In no special order, please consider enemies, escapes, and pests.

Pests include wild birds, mice, and small children. A young mouse, for instance, can sometimes squeeze

While Society Finches and Gouldians are compatible species, the gregarious Societies may hinder the Gouldians' attempts at breeding.

through half-inch-square wire mesh and, by scurrying around at night, rob your birds of sleep and even cause them to hurt themselves as they blindly fly into objects in the dark. Your birds will not thrive if they are harassed at night by mice or other creatures. You must ensure them a quiet night, every night. Make up your mind before you invest too much cash or time: do you want to maintain a collection of healthy birds, or do you wish to show them off to all comers—smokers, coughers, sneezers, cage rattlers, shouters, and arm wavers included?

Escapes are easy for all finches. They are inquiring, probing, searching, all the day long. If an opening one inch in diameter exists anywhere, they will find it and be out even if they didn't really want to go anywhere in particular. If you build an aviary, make the doors as low as you can conveniently bend under. Many escapes take place over your head when a high door is opened. Corridors and arrangements of double doors are ideal for the prevention of escapes. The drawback is that you have to open and close twice as many doors in order to make a visit.

Most dogs, virtually all cats, rats, and some parasitic arthropods are genuine enemies of caged birds. There is no such thing as a safe cat. No prudent bird keeper trusts cats. And in case you wondered, fleas, mites, and ticks and lice are all parasitic arthropods. In case you wondered further, an ideal parasite lives off another animal without killing it. Finally, an arthropod is an invertebrate with jointed legs.

VISITORS

You should be seen by your finches. Visit them daily, during the light hours. If you breed a few, handle the babies once their eyes are open if only to put bands on them. These birds have been with humans for a long time, and they seem to get along well with us. They will not become as intimate with you as a budgie or a parrot, but as you care for your birds, you will notice that you are trusted. We all know (and birds know instinctively) that they are vulnerable when they bathe. It is not easy to take off from a muddy, wet surface, and it is not possible to fly at top speed with wet feathers. Nevertheless, your birds will bathe while you watch them.

Cage birds do well with routine. So create a routine and then stick to it. Cage cleaning, feeding, nest inspection, and casual visits should all be done during the bright-light hours, regardless of whether the light is daylight or artificial. Don't let daylight dim and then suddenly turn on brilliant electric lights and expect your birds to appreciate your company. Most cage birds will probably tolerate the shock, but rare or delicate species could easily keel over after a few such experiences.

Noise is also a problem you will have to cope with. Again, your birds will adjust to conditions which build up gradually and then repeat themselves at predictable intervals. Look at birds and bats in a church belfry. All day long the bell rings every hour on the hour, but the bats sleep right through. All night long the clanging continues, but the birds never fluster.

When frightened, your aviary birds will fly toward the light, and if the light happens to be coming through a glass window, broken necks and fractured skulls could result. Usually prevention is easy to accomplish. Stretch a cheeseclothlike fabric over the inside of the window and fasten it to the frame with thumbtacks or staples. Most of the light will still get in, but collisions will be cushioned. Another alternative is to "paint" the window glass inside with a powder-type cleanser or calcimine whitewash. These materials, even if applied thinly, will suffice to warn the birds. Of course, the cheesecloth offers real protection; the painting is merely a warning.

CATCHING BIRDS

Properly managed, caged Gouldians are usually so tame that with a little practice you can pick them up in your hand. If you can't, you had better find out why they are scary. Check for (and eliminate) flashing lights at night, rodents, cats, dogs, sudden noises, and other irritants of a similar nature.

Aviary birds are usually less tame than cage birds, and you will probably need a net to capture them for banding or caging. A walk-in aviary of, say, a thousand cubic feet needs no more than a ten- or twelve-inch-diameter net. Buy it from a bird dealer, professional net maker, or from

The blue breast, evident in the bird above and on the facing page, is inherited independently of head color. This variety is still novel and not frequently seen.

Gouldians fare well in a roomy cage; three cubic feet is suitable for two birds. This model features a removable tray, which makes cleaning the cage easier, and a side opening, which allows breeding birds to enter an external nest box that can be fastened to the side of the cage.

a pet shop that handles birds. The fabric in the commercial nets has been chosen for its mesh size and stiffness. It's not likely that you can take precisely the right fabric from an old curtain or find it in a store. By the time you get the right hoop and the right dowel and the ferrule and the pattern, you could have bought a dozen better nets and saved money. I know because I tried.

The net handle in a walk-in hundred-square-foot aviary need be no longer than eighteen inches. The hoop might well be bound with a soft spongy material to reduce the risk of injury to the birds. This is something you *can* do, since most store-bought nets are not so cushioned.

Ideally, to catch a bird, work at dusk or in subdued light. Remember that a frightened bird will fly toward the light. Also, and this is really an important thing to note, each bird will establish its own pattern of flight between perches. Once you determine the pattern for the bird you wish to catch, stand ready at one of the stopping points—a window sill perhaps—and then get the bird to fly from some other perch. When it arrives where your net is poised at the ready, take the bird instantly. The moment of its landing is the moment it is not prepared to go elsewhere. If you doubt this, ask any duck hunter. Don't try to catch a bird in midflight; this is how birds end up with broken wings. Once the bird is netted, remove it by hand and quickly transfer it to a carton, holding cage, or whatever. Your technique will improve with practice. If you are clumsy, practice with Zebra Finches before you get involved with more delicate or more expensive species.

In line with catching birds, limit yourself to "exotic" cage birds. Do not trap or possess any wild finches native to the U.S.A. It is against federal law to own or traffic in most native wild birds. A Philadelphia lawyer might find a few loopholes, but a Philadelphia judge might find the lawyer was wrong. So, just don't catch or keep protected native birds. Stay out of jail—this is on the federal statute books as a felony!

A White-breasted Yellow-headed male (*above*), a rare color variety.
A Red-headed male with the normal purple breast (*facing page*).
Except for the facial area and breast, the other areas are colored
the same.

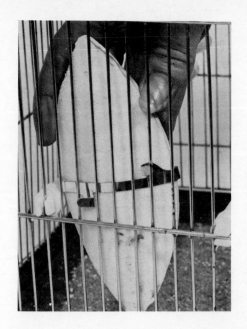

Cuttlebone (*left*) is a source of calcium for Gouldians, and it serves as a tool for sharpening their beaks. *Below:* Seedeating birds often drop the seed hulls right in their food dishes, so it is important to blow off the chaff from time to time to expose the remaining seed.

Feeding and Watering

FOOD

Gouldian Finches in cages and aviaries eat and thrive on the same fare as the other small Australian, African, and Indian seedeating finches like Zebras and Cut-throats and Societies. The basic diet item of these birds in captivity is millet, and it should be supplemented with canary seed, spray millet, poppy, sesame, rape, and hemp. With the exception of my remarks about termites, this chapter is applicable to the feeding of all seedeating caged finches. If your Gouldian is in a cage or aviary with perhaps Zebras, Societies, nuns, Green Singing Finches, cordonbleus, or other similar species, this one package of advice is applicable to all of them. Push the minerals, charcoal, cuttlebone, hard-boiled egg and its shell, grit, and especially a square of fresh, grassy garden sod. Provide ample fresh water daily for bathing and drinking. Your birds will bathe in their drinking water and drink their bath water; however, your job is simply to provide fresh, clean water

for all their needs.

Yes, Gouldian Finch diet in the cage or aviary is simple, but because it is simple, this doesn't mean it can be neglected. No finch can live on a single kind of seed and lettuce alone, however much it may enjoy these things. The basic building block in the diet of your finches is millet, so let's consider it first. There are several varieties and sizes of millet in the marketplace, and you may find that the best source of seed is your pet shop, where you can obtain one-pound cartons of a "finch mixture." This consists of millet, canary, rape, niger, oats, and perhaps other seeds as well. If you have more than thirty birds, then you should be getting your millet in bulk, perhaps 25 or even 50 pounds at a time. Which millet should you feed to Gouldian Finches? Try a few and settle for the one or two they favor. The sizes and colors vary, but the nutrient value of all millets are about the same. Most of the color in millet is in the hull, and your bird will remove the millet hull before it eats the kernel anyway. So, don't take color too seriously.

Although millet is the basic dietary ingredient for seedeating finches, its protein content is lower than what your Gouldian Finches ideally should have. One problem is that millet lacks certain amino acids. This is why experienced bird keepers will offer a variety of oily seeds including rape, niger, poppy, and sesame to supplement the basic millet diet. In case you wondered why oily seeds are recommended to increase protein in the diet, it is a fact that most high-fat seeds are also high in protein. Canary seed, a notable exception, is a good protein source even though it is not relatively high in oil.

Interestingly, canary seed (*Phalaris canariensis*) just happens to be high in those amino acids which are correspondingly low in millet (*Panicum miliaceum*). It should also be mentioned here that spray millet is in fact not a *Panicum* but is classified in another genus of plants and is scientifically called *Setaria italica*.

Nutrient values will vary with the minerals and fertilizers in the soil, growth rate, and rainfall, but even so, they do serve to explain why experienced breeders will offer more than just millet to their birds. It has been suggested that protein, especially for breeding finches, should amount to about 19% of the diet. Actually, when the Gouldian shucks the hull from millet, its fiber content will go down several percentage points and protein will increase.

The following tabulation has been adopted from data found in Winton, *The Structure and Composition of Foods* (1939) and Petrak, *Diseases of Cage and Aviary Birds* (1969).

Seed, including hull	Protein	Fat	Fiber	Ash	Carbo-hydrate*
Rice	8	2	9	5	65
Oats	12	4	12	3	58
Millet	13	2	9	4	62
Canary Seed	14	4	21	10	27
Spray Millet	15	6	11	6	51
Sunflower	15	28	29	3	17
Fennel	16	12	14	9	32
Niger	19	43	14	3	12
Rape	20	45	6	4	18
Caraway	20	17	16	7	29
Poppy	21	50	5	7	10
Sesame	21	47	5	6	19
Hemp	22	30	19	5	16
Gold of Pleasure	22	31	11	7	22
Flax	24	37	6	4	22

Carbohydrate other than fiber

SPRAY MILLET

Experienced bird fanciers are happy to buy spray millet for their birds for more than two dollars per pound, and in small quantities they will pay as much as three dollars a pound! They know that their birds love it. Try this simple test; I already did. Release your birds in a large, sunny aviary and let them settle down. Some will bathe, others will roost, still others will pick at grit, preen, build nests, or simply fly back and forth. There will be little or no uniform activity, especially if there are several species present. Then put a few stalks of spray millet in a weighted vase or hang a bundle from a wire; within minutes *all* the birds of all the species will be picking over that spray millet.

Should the price of "over-two-dollars-per-pound" bother you, try taking an autumn walk through a field. With a shopping bag and a pair of snippers, you can gather all sorts of weeds that are going to seed. If you want your seed gathering expedition to be scientific you should read two paperback Dover reprints: Martin, Zim, and Nelson, *American Wildlife and Plants* (1961) and Knobel, *Field Guide to the Grasses, Sedges, and Rushes of the U.S.* (1977).

Both of these books point out that spray millet, or foxtail millet, or bristlegrass, or *Setaria italica,* is the same species, whether domesticated or wild. The trouble is that it may have been sprayed with a poison. If you purchase a domestic, commercially grown product, you have the right to assume that it was not treated with any dangerous insecticide or herbicide. You pay your money and you take your choice.

Buy clean seed—not damp, not water stained, not musty or moldy. It may have some webs in it, and if you watch patiently, you may see movement. Not quite as much as the movement of Mexican jumping beans, but movement nevertheless. The webs and the movement mean that there are little white- or creamy-colored grubs, or larvae, in your birdseed. These larvae—many people call them web worms—are perhaps as large around as a pencil-lead and about five-eighths of an inch long. They have a cylindrical body with two rows of legs—much like a tiny inchworm, only they creep rather than inch about in the seed. Don't worry about a few of them; the birds might just eat them along with the seeds. Later the larvae will pupate in cocoons, and small moths will emerge to continue the cycle of life.

Remember that your birds are locked in your cage with a basic diet of millet which you bought from a pet dealer who bought it from a distributor who bought it from a wholesale grain merchant who bought it from a farmer who might have neglected to fertilize his millet field when he planted the seed. A wild bird sensing a lack of an essential nutrient will search it out. When you keep a captive bird, you have voluntarily assumed an obligation to provide at least as much. Although—and this bears repeating—Gouldian Finches can live out normal lives with minerals, grit, water, and millet, this is much like a jailbird on bread and water: he will survive. Period.

Advice about offering small quantities when introducing

Although Gouldian Finches love spray millet, it is a somewhat expensive treat.

a "new" food is good advice for any supplement or treat or diet change for any captive bird. As a precaution, if you plan to add or subtract an item from the diet of your birds, do it long before they begin to breed. They should be thoroughly accustomed to the food they are getting before they begin to feed their babies. For example, you may have neglected to provide grit until the eggs hatch. Well, that's too bad, but something even worse would happen if you suddenly introduced grit at that time. The adults in blissful ignorance might pump a fatal dose of indigestible grit into the crop of a newly hatched chick. A "precaution" is a caution you should consider in advance of an emergency or a catastrophe. So do that.

You will probably find that you cannot teach your birds to eat anything, but if they see another bird doing it, they will learn rapidly. For example, if your Gouldians will not touch a mealworm or a fly maggot, but have a cordonbleu that does eat these things, you might cage the birds together for perhaps a week. Your Gouldians may do for another bird what they won't do for you.

Be careful to distinguish between seeds and seed hulls. Many a beginning fancier has starved his or her birds by mistaking empty hulls for whole seeds. Some fanciers dump the feed dishes on schedule and start anew with fresh seed daily. Others winnow the seed with a small machine which is available through specialized bird supply houses. Still others winnow seed by blowing on it, which is a dusty bother and may be dangerous to your health. One neat and economical approach is to dump the uneaten seed and hulls on a damp turkish towel or onto a dish of damp earth, and then the uneaten grain will soak and germinate and sprout while the birds pick it over.

Living seed undergoes chemical changes when it germinates, and in this state it becomes a beneficial supplement to the basic dry millet. This is especially valuable when feeding birds which are, in turn, feeding nestlings. For each bird involved, soak one-half teaspoon of the same seed you are presently feeding in room-temperature tap water for twenty-four hours and then spread it out on a damp towel for an additional twenty-four hours. Now call this product "half-germinated" seed and feed it to your birds and especially to nestlings. Let the same seed remain on the damp towel for several days more and call it "sprouted" seed, also excellent as a diet supplement for your birds. Let them eat as much of it as they wish after you accustom them to it over the course of a week or so of offering only small quantities.

To increase the protein content of your Gouldians' diet—especially if they are breeding—you would be well advised to add egg. Hard-boil one for thirty minutes, then dice it with a fork or push it through a strainer (also feed them the shell).

In their native Australia, Gouldians are known to eat termites, but few American bird keepers get their birds to eat this natural, high-protein dietary supplement. Termites and silkworm pupae are nutritionally excellent but a bother to prepare. You can buy them from your pet dealer or through advertisements in the bird magazines. More easily available are mealworms; try feeding only the soft, recently molted ones.

Offer greens of all kinds: dandelion, lettuce, spinach, celery tops. If it is good for them, they may eat it. If it is not good, they certainly will not eat it. Note: they *may* eat it—and then, they may not.

Another supplement your birds may benefit from is dried seaweed. It is high in minerals, and they may have a craving for it if a trace element is otherwise lacking in their diet. If your birds will eat peanut butter, butter, or margarine consider yourself fortunate; they are all excellent sources of edible oil. Offer it to them spread on a piece of bread or toast or pound cake. Powdered yeast will stick to seed which has been moistened with cod-liver oil; this concoction is a high-fat, high-protein, high-vitamin-D supplement that your birds can well be given occasionally.

Among the supplements which your finches may enjoy are honey and oranges. You might offer a slice of bread or toast which was moistened with a mixture of honey and orange juice or perhaps just one or the other. Gouldians caged with Gouldians might refuse this treat; but Gouldians caged with munias or Societies or Zebras might quickly learn to love it.

Do you know how to make french toast? Most recipes contain milk and beaten eggs soaked into bread which is then fried in butter or margarine on a griddle. Here is a high-protein, high-fat, high-vitamin food supplement. Your birds will eat it as avidly and as frequently as you do.

Do you usually put just a little honey on it? That's how caged finches like it. Bear in mind, as always, that millet is their basic food. French toast is not a substitute; it is a supplement.

A food supplement you can prepare from a proven formula is worth trying, especially if you have more than fifty birds. For a very small collection, the effort is hard to justify, so you would probably be better off with something from your pet shop. This supplemental feeding method was adapted from one developed by Hylton Blythe, Thorpe Bay, Essex, England and first published in the *Avicultural Magazine,* 1957, p. 65.

> 1 lb. bread rusk—this is a bread which has been sliced and then baked crisp in an oven at relatively low heat.
>
> 2 oz. powdered dry skim milk
>
> 1 oz. wheat germ

1 oz. bran

1 oz. peanut oil

1 oz. cod-liver oil.

Mix the two oils and combine with the crushed rusk. Then add the other ingredients, mix, and store in a tin or refrigerate until required. Then, moisten with water and feed only what the birds will clean up in a few hours.

This formula is obviously higher in fat and protein and vitamins A, B, and D than a diet of millet and canary seeds. Herein lies its benefit to your birds. Remember, this does not provide grit or minerals; these must come from other sources. Also remember that all the supplements in the world are still only supplements. The basic diet of the caged Gouldian Finch is still millet.

GRIT

Small birds hull seeds, but larger species like pigeons, poultry, and waterfowl do not. Gouldian Finches, like virtually all seedeaters, swallow kernels whole. There is no chewing in the mouth; this is accomplished later in a powerfully muscular organ located beyond the crop, the gizzard. Here the kernels and an assortment of bits of gravel are squeezed and churned and ground until the seeds break up into a mass of damp flour, which is subsequently digested.

The bird will swallow only as much grit as it senses that it needs. Your pet shop, bird store, or nearby beach will furnish a supply. You may also discover that your Gouldians will eat charcoal, oyster shell, cuttlebone, and eggshells. Good!—but these are not substitutes for gravel. However, some recognized authorities believe that seedeating cage birds do not need grit and actually do better without it. Others disagree. Until all the facts are in, I remain neutral and leave the decision to you.

VITAMINS AND MINERALS

Novice bird keepers sometimes neglect the few mandatory and vital things because bird keeping looks so absurdly simple. A good example for this is neglect of your birds' mineral requirements. No bird, especially a relatively delicate species like the Gouldian, can survive for long without minerals, but individuals can go for long periods without *ingesting* any. If a critical nutritional element is missing, the existing supply stored in bones or blood or certain organs will be gradually depleted, and the loss to the bird will take place so insidiously that you may never realize that sterility or poor plumage or death is imminent. The classic example of this has to do with the horse which was gradually trained to eat pure sawdust. The trouble was that the beast dropped dead just when it looked as though the experiment was a success.

Your birds should have a mineral block or mineral-grit mixture or some other source of minerals before them at all times. It should be placed where it is accessible, but not so that it will be covered with droppings. There is no sense for you to make up this mineral mixture—there are plenty of good ones available from pet shops and bird supply houses. The major ingredients are sodium chloride (common salt) and calcium carbonate (limestone). The other ingredients are present as traces and include iron, copper, potassium, phosphorus, sulfur, iodine, and even that notorious poison, arsenic. All animal life, man included, requires virtually all the chemically reactive elements in carefully proportioned traces. For birds, some will come from the seed, some will be found in water, vegetables, eggs, or bread, or other food supplements you provide, and some may not be there. The mineral block or mineral grit is an inexpensive insurance policy. Cuttlebone is both a beak sharpener and a good source of calcium plus a few other important trace elements, but cuttlebone is not a substitute for good mineral block or grit, properly proportioned to supply all the minerals and trace elements your birds need.

You may discover that the broken shells of the hard-boiled eggs you feed to your birds are favored over cuttlebone. This is great, so long as those shells were boiled for at least one-half hour—or baked over low heat in the oven. The reason is that some avian diseases are transmitted by way of raw eggs. A second reason is that it is not a good idea to suggest to a bird that raw birds' eggs are good bird food. So, if you find that your birds crave even more shell than they get with their ration of hard-boiled eggs, save the shells from home cooking, but remember to boil or bake them for a half-hour before feeding.

You may wish to buy some additional insurance in the form of liquid vitamins. Some successful breeders swear by vitamins, others consider them not too important. I never used them. Probably an unsupplemented diet of millet needs a vitamin-and-mineral boost, but a broad-based menu (including hard-boiled eggs; fresh greens like kale, spinach, green lettuce, carrot tops, and grass cuttings; fruit; whole-wheat bread; oatmeal; rape, niger, and poppy seeds and wild-bird mixtures from time to time) will eliminate the need for vitamin supplements.

The subject of vitamins is controversial. Perhaps it deserves some more amplification and a little philosophizing. The more you paid for your bird, the more likely you are to pump it up with nutritional supplements. Since you probably laid out more for your Gouldian than for any other finch, you are fair game for every supplement product that ever came down the pike. You can be reasonably sure that the labels on the package are correct. Reputable manufacturers of food products sold in pet shops don't lie about the ingredients.

Food supplements ensure an adequate supply of what should naturally be in fresh, wholesome, natural bird food. So why use them? Because you want to be *certain*. Great!—but choose just *one*. Pick one with a large number of ingredients and offer it as a *supplement* to the best quality and widest variety of foods your birds will accept. It is unnecessary to accumulate a collection of remedies and aids to keep your Gouldian healthy.

The list which follows is a brief review of the names of the vitamins, their natural sources, and the diseases of birds which develop when these substances are absent from the diet.

• Vitamin A: Found in eggs and green vegetables, it improves night vision and resistance to infection, especially of skin. It is possible that excessive dosing of vitamin A causes french molt in budgies.

• Vitamin B: This is the famous beriberi–nerve-disease vitamin. Actually there are a dozen or so B vitamins, found mostly in proteins and yeast. Niacin is vital for growth and good plumage.

- Vitamin C: This is the scurvy-citrus-fruit vitamin, also called ascorbic acid. Seedeating birds seem to manufacture it and so do not require any in their diet.
- Vitamin D: Calcium metabolism depends on vitamin D, and the source of it is ultraviolet radiation on some oils and fats. Birds in direct sunlight make their own vitamin D.
- Vitamin E: Found in seed germs, it is destroyed through oxidation by excessive dosage of cod-liver oil. Believed to improve fertility.
- Vitamin K: Required for coagulation of blood. Produced in the intestines by bacteria and so not required in the diet. Vitamin K is especially vulnerable to antibiotics.
- Biotin: Improves hatchability of eggs.

Vitamins A, D, and E and K are soluble in fat and are often associated with oily or fatty foods. Vitamins B and C are soluble in water.

Be aware that indiscriminate dosing of cage birds with antibiotics can actually destroy vitamins or reduce the bird's ability to assimilate the vitamins it does ingest.

One aspect of nutrition, well-known but frequently overlooked by beginners in aviculture, is that calcium in cuttlebone and egg shells requires vitamin D in order to be properly utilized. That is the reason that milk, a high-calcium food, is often fortified with vitamin D. This vitamin D, then, is antirachitic, or the preventive for rickets, the disease of soft bones. Vitamin D, a natural chemical substance, is often called the sunlight vitamin because it is so closely tied in with solar rays. In fact, the process for making the vitamin D in milk hinges on irradiation of fats by certain wave lengths of ultraviolet light naturally emitted by the sun or artificially created by special electrical-discharge lamps. The point is simply that direct, unfiltered sunlight seems to help birds to produce vitamin D. So, you should, if possible, give your birds the advantage of a screened aviary, part of which is exposed to direct sunlight at least a few hours daily. A more sophisticated technique would be to provide ultraviolet light from a lamp—this is difficult and expensive, and it could be dangerous if overdone. The third method is to provide foods and food supplements which are known to be rich in the various complex fractions of this important substance. You may, if you wish, supplement your finchs' diet by adding irradiated cod-liver oil to some of the seed you feed, or you might use a vitamin-D concentrate available from your pet dealer or pharmacist. As you can see, there are several routes to follow; choose the one that is most convenient and don't neglect it.

As an aside to people who avoid eating foods containing cholesterol, it should be pointed out that as long ago as 1924, studies of cholesterol and vitamin D showed that "cholesterol, which accompanies most animal fats, and the analogous constituents of vegetable oils, became active antirachitically when exposed to ultraviolet radiation." This quotation is from the fourteenth edition of the *Encyclopaedia Britannica*. Actually, it is not the cholesterol itself that is activated but a minor component associated with it and known as ergosterol. Don't worry that cholesterol in your birds' diet will cause heart disease. It is very likely that by the time you read this book there will be ample evidence to prove that the quantity of cholesterol that plugs the circulatory system of your pet bird or yourself has nothing to do with the quantity of cholesterol in the diet. Animals and people manufacture cholesterol regardless of what they eat.

The other vitamins necessary for the health and fertility of your birds (A, B, C, and E) will come naturally if you show intelligent care in providing fresh, raw green vegetables, a variety of live seeds (test them occasionally to be sure they sprout) and dietary supplements such as fruit, hard-boiled eggs, scrambled eggs, and wheat germ. The supplemental foods are especially important for Gouldian Finches. As I mentioned previously, wild Gouldians in Australia eat large numbers of flying termites—something that caged birds are not likely to encounter. I daresay most cage-bred Gouldian Finches would not spontaneously eat a termite if one were offered.

SEED STORAGE

If you store more than a pound of seed, and to avoid the nuisance of mice, web worms, mealworms, or other vermin, consider the use and convenience of the plastic milk container. It is free, easy to clean, easy to fill by the use of a funnel, and easy to seal. With it, moisture content and loss to insects will be under your control. A label with the description and source of the seed is easy to affix; additionally, you quickly can judge how much you have on hand. Don't store seed in bright sunlight; the light and heat may degrade the nutrient values. These bottles are also handy for water if you have no plumbing in your aviary or bird room. (An open bucket of water is an invitation to disaster by drowning.) Just rinse the bottles thoroughly and don't neglect washing the caps.

Except for hemp, which has been deliberately killed to keep it out of the marijuana-cultivation business, *all* bird seed should be capable of germinating. You should test your seed to ensure that it is alive. Plant some as you would lawn seed, or put some on a wet towel for a few days to be sure that at least 75% of it sprouts. Properly stored, bird seed should remain alive for several years.

WATER FOR DRINKING AND BATHING

Some diseases and parasites your birds may have or may get are often transmitted from one bird to another when fecal matter gets into their food or drinking water. This is something you must (and easily can) control. Don't arrange the cage or aviary so that a perch is located over another perch or over food or water. Do change water dishes frequently and do wash them thoroughly before you refill them.

Chlorine is frequently added to municipal water supplies to reduce odors and to reduce the possibility of transmission of diseases. Some birds tolerate small amounts, but others seem to resent it. Fortunately, chlorine escapes to the air if water is left standing with a large surface exposed. Agitation helps. Boiling helps, but it really is unnecessary. If your water is heavily chlorinated, simply draw off what you need into gallon plastic milk bottles. Fill only up to the level where the bottle begins to narrow down—say, three quarts—and let it stand, uncorked, for a day or two. Hot tap water will give up chlorine even faster. Let it stand while it cools, then use it.

Water temperature is not critical. Serve it at room temperature or, if it is cooler, it will soon reach room temperature. The same goes for bath water. Some Gouldians will bathe twice daily if you leave water out for them. (Incidentally, this is where an anodized aluminum, rustproof cage earns its keep. Generally the tray or the bottom of the cage gets punishment from grit, bird droppings, and water.) Gouldian Finches like to have bathing water close by at all times. A tray or glass dish one-inch deep and as large as possible is what they need. The water depth should be about one-half inch. If the sides of the tray are but one-half inch deep, the loss of water due to splashing will make a mess. If the tray is much deeper than one inch, the birds will be inhibited, probably because the bath tub will seem too much like a trap. The birds want to jump in and fly out easily.

Don't expect juvenile Gouldian Finches to bathe until they are fully fledged—three months would be about the youngest age at which they will voluntarily go into the water, and a month more or less will not make any difference to the health of your bird.

If you have been offering water to your adult birds from a dish deeper than one-half inch, remove it when fledglings leave the nest to avert the risk of their drowning. As a matter of fact, as I mentioned before, a one-half-inch water depth is adequate for any finch to bathe in.

Don't get the idea that because you furnish a drinking-water dish and a bath-water dish they will use these facilities that way. There always will be a bath-water drinker and a drinking-water bather. Don't fight it. Just try to keep all the water clean and fresh.

That dish of bath water will teach you a lot about your birds. Watch it. Remember that they are inveterate bathers. If each adult does not take a dip (or two) every day, look closely at the water. It probably is not clean enough for *you* to want to drink. Rinse out the dish and fill it with fresh, clean, cool water, and most likely all those birds will be in it up to their rumps within minutes.

If your Gouldian Finches are provided with a bath, and the water is fresh and clean, and still they don't use it, look to its depth. These little fellows are pretty fussy about how far to wade in before splashing. The simplest procedure is for you to provide a long bath tub, raise one end an inch, and fill the tub until the high end is barely wet. Then, somewhere over that sloped bottom, the water depth will be precisely what the birds prefer. Try it, they'll like it!

If you house your birds in an outdoor aviary, you may

discover that they capture ants and rub themselves with them, or that they stand over an anthill and permit the ants to crawl over themselves. The ants are of the nonstinging varieties, and the birds known to do this include 200 species in 30 of the 56 passerine families. Whether Gouldians also indulge is for you to find out. At this moment, positive evidence is lacking.

If your birds do it, at least we think we know why. It seems that formic acid and other similar chemicals generated by many species of ants will keep lice away. Other liquids produced by ants may aid in feather maintenance. Among the Estrildidae, waxbills are known to "ant," and we know that some waxbills are related to the Australian finches, so you can go on from there.

Dust bathing is another activity your birds may indulge in if you provide the ingredients. Bone-dry fine sand or earth is worked into the plumage and then it is shaken out, perhaps for feather maintenance or perhaps for louse control. Some species bathe first in dust and then in water when the situation permits. The common House Sparrow (*Passer domesticus*) is a good example.

Sunbathing is another form of bathing that all finches will indulge in whenever the opportunity affords. Really, they are very busy "doing things" all the daylight hours. But they are opportunists, and when the sun shines, they will spread their feathers and soak in some sun rays. If the sunlight gets to your birds through a glass window, it will have lost that vitally important ingredient, ultraviolet.

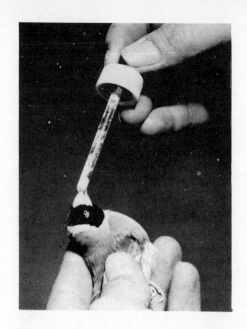

If a Gouldian becomes sick, medicine can be administered with an eye dropper (*left*). A pair of Gouldians with their three youngsters (*below*). If one of the family members shows signs of illness, it should be removed to a hospital cage and kept isolated and extra warm.

Illness and Care

DISEASE

Start with healthy birds from a reliable source. Gouldian Finches are relatively expensive, but a "cheap" bird is no bargain. Feed them good millet and supplement the millet with other seeds, green vegetables, minerals, grit, and clean water. Don't introduce sick birds or birds that haven't been in quarantine of some sort. Let them sleep all night, every night, without interruption. Give them sufficient room.

All right, you did all that. Now enjoy your birds; chances are good they will never have a sick day. But what if they do? First, go over the checklist of food, water, shelter—the basics. Then evaluate the damage. Did you lose one bird simply because it flew into a window and broke its neck, or is there an epidemic in your aviary? Look for signs: ruffled feathers, eyes appearing small, much daytime sleeping, little eating, wet vents, running nostrils, no chirping. You will have to be a detective, because most bird diseases are

hard to diagnose positively without an autopsy. Do the obvious thing first: see a veterinarian and be prepared to pay for the visit. He may have to work as hard on your bird as he does on Fifi the poodle.

Second, study the diseases of birds in a specialized book. There are several. Robert (Birdman of Alcatraz) Stroud's *Diseases of Canaries* (T.F.H. Publications) is applicable. Another scholarly text used by veterinarians and advanced bird keepers is Arnall and Keymer, *Bird Diseases* (also published by T.F.H.).

FEATHER PLUCKING

Do not confuse natural, normal molting with feather plucking. The molt is a seasonal, summertime thing. The molting bird does not end up with bald spots—it just looks a bit ragged for several weeks. Feather plucking is a vice. Some birds do it to other birds. Isolate the offender, and the victim or victims will recover in a month or two. Some birds do it to themselves. Frequently the cause is overcrowding or lack of minerals, especially salt, in the diet. These are things you can correct.

Sometimes mites are the irritant, and the bird tears out its feathers as it scratches its sore spots. Your pet-supply store probably handles antiplucking sprays that can be applied to the victim. They are frequently effective, but you should search out the cause and correct it rather than go after only the symptoms.

If you have a pair with an aggressive male and an uncooperative female, you may be witnessing some prenuptial funny-business. This generally shows up as a loss of feathers on the back of the neck of the female. She probably will recover completely and go on to raise a big, healthy family.

SOFT MOLT

If you are inconsistent about the cage lighting and heating and do not establish a pattern for hours of light and hours of darkness, the metabolic process of your birds will be affected adversely. In plain language, they will molt out of season. This condition is termed "soft molt." The bird in soft molt never looks quite right. Its feathers will always be ragged, and its overall appearance will look wrong to you. Even if you can't put your finger on the problem precisely, you will just know something is not quite right. When this happens to you, you are changing from a bird owner to a bird keeper. But that doesn't help your bird. What the bird needs is a carefully controlled astronomical clock to turn the lights on early every day or turn them off late every night so that the cage is illuminated at *regular* intervals of about thirteen hours on and eleven hours off. Remember that Gouldian Finches come from the tropics, where the days are always long. If this supplement to daylight is on a simple on-off clock switch, it should be accompanied by a dim night light so the birds are never stranded in total darkness when that clock turns the bright light off.

MOLTING

Your healthy, normal birds will probably molt once a year, beginning in July or August and continuing for about two months. They will never be unable to fly or appear bald or naked. A feather here, a feather there—you won't miss them, but you will notice them on the floor. Don't fuss with special foods to carry the birds through the molt—if they are properly nourished, they will manage to manufacture a few feathers from what they have been eating all along. If a feather grows in twisted or broken, you may want to pluck it rather than wait a year for the next molt. If you pull a feather, it will be replaced in less than a month.

CLAWS

The normal length of the four claws on each foot is perhaps one-sixteenth or one-eighth inch longer than the part with a blood supply in it. If the claws grow corkscrewed or overly long, perching and even hopping will become difficult. Should such a long-clawed bird attempt to incubate a clutch of eggs, it will surely puncture a few. Clip the claws with a fingernail clipper or small, sharp scissors. You will be able to see the blood vessels when you look through the claws toward the light. Clip one-sixteenth inch beyond the end of this pink portion. If you inadvertently draw blood (really this is unnecessary), touch the end of the claw with a styptic pencil or a little alum powder, and the slight bleeding will immediately stop. Many birds go through their years of life with no claw clipping, so you need not do it on a routine basis, but rather on an as-needed basis.

BROKEN LIMBS

Once in a while a finch will break a leg or a wing. Many bird keepers have kept hundreds of finches for decades and never had it happen, but it might. If this occurs as a result of frail bones caused by a calcium deficiency, you should look to minerals and vitamin D. If the problem is in the cage design, the answer will be obvious.

What to do with the injured bird? You decide, but here are a few hints and guidelines. Splints consisting of a one-quarter by three-eighths-inch piece of transparent household mending tape have been used with success by some fanciers. A hospital cage with no perches, quiet isolation, warmth, and rest sometimes will suffice for spontaneous mending of a broken bone. Amputation is only rarely necessary. One-legged birds will thrive for their normal life span, but they will not breed, since both legs are necessary for a bird to keep its balance during copulation.

Wings are even less frequently broken, and they generally mend within three weeks in a hospital cage with quiet isolation. There is not much you can do about a broken wing on a finch, but if you wish to go to the expense, you might consult your veterinarian.

THE HOSPITAL CAGE

Your birds should go through life without ever being sick. Ideally, the only time you might need to touch a Gouldian Finch would be to clip its claws or to band its leg.

If you should acquire an ill bird or if an accident should befall a bird, your primary action should be to provide *isolation* and *warmth*. Buy or build a hospital cage. It need not be very large. A fifteen-inch cube will suffice. It should have a low perch, a water and a food supply, and *controlled* warmth. Controlled warmth is a big item in the cure of most cage-bird ailments, and for Gouldians especially, 85 or 90 F. is what they need; they are tropicals. In the event of a broken leg, remove the perch from the cage until the bone has mended.

A heater should be coupled with an adjustable thermostat. The ideal arrangements for this have long since been worked out and are available through pet dealers. If you feel you cannot afford the manufactured product, look at one and adapt the design. The best source of heat is electricity—25 watts will probably suffice, 50 would be more than ample. The adjustable feature of the thermostat is important, because after the bird recovers from its ailment, the temperature should be lowered to that of the normal room gradually, over the course of several additional days before ending the treatment. For egg binding, colds, constipation, and general malaise, begin with warmth and then treat the specific illness, if you are able to recognize it.

TWO SPECIAL PRECAUTIONS

If you are interested in adding birds from another bird room or aviary, do it only if you are absolutely sure of the health of the new birds. If in doubt, isolate the newcomers for at least two weeks, preferably in another building, at least in another room. Don't be the carrier of disease as you go from newly introduced birds to your own valued stock.

A bird can kill itself by a broken neck or fractured skull if it flies full speed ahead into a closed window. *If* your aviary has some glass windows, you may discover that frightened birds fly into them. Spray a little whitewash or paint on each window pane so that it doesn't look like the great outdoors, and the birds will avoid it.

COMPANIONS AND PESTS

Birds may also be bothered by certain cage companions you should eliminate. These are the many species of jointed-leg creatures. Here we consider the animals in the phylum Arthropoda, including the class Insecta and the class Arachnida. Among the insects are found mosquitoes, flies, and lice. The arachnids include mites, ticks, and spiders. In both classes there are some scavengers and some parasites. "Some" is the wrong word—there are hundreds of species, some known, some unkown, some large enough to swat, others so small you need a microscope to merely see them and a high-power microscope to examine them. Don't bother; it will get you nowhere.

Bird lice are a minor irritant which you can control, but

many species of mites and all ticks are genuine enemies which you must actively fight. Fortunately, the life-style of the parasitic mite helps you win the battle against it. It is a nocturnal feeder. During the night the mite sucks blood, and during the day it hides and deposits its eggs in the crevices and cracks of nest boxes. So, during the daylight hours, your birds are free of mites, and you should take advantage of this fact. Place a white cotton cloth over the cage of birds in the evening before you retire. Examine it the following morning. Mites will have crawled off the birds and settled in the folds of the cloth. Good. Fold up the cloth and burn it. In the morning you should put the mite-infested birds into a cage you recently sterilized with washing soda and boiling water, then sterilize the cage they had been in. Get into all the hiding places in the aviary with gamma benzene hexachloride. Do this once every ten days for three or four cycles, and you will have wiped out most or all of the mites. Then do it once every month or sooner if the mites show up again.

Ticks need to be picked off by hand or with tweezers; they can also be controlled by chemicals. Lice, mosquitoes, and flies will succumb to pyrethrum compounds, paradichlorobenzene, or a No-Pest strip used intermittently. Remember that a light spray or dusting of pyrethrum is safe for all birds, including these finches, but too much exposure to a No-Pest strip or to gamma benzene hexachloride might possibly be dangerous. If convenient, move the birds out while any high-powered insecticide is working.

Paradichlorobenzene, the famous clothes-moth control, is effective against lice and mites. Now and then put some crystals near a louse-infested cage for a few days and if the treatment proves effective, continue it.

Some bird keepers report that they control lice with a spray they make up. It contains one part of Listerine and four parts of witch hazel. However, there is not now and probably never will be one certain, cut-and-dried, sure control for all pests and parasites.

Among the thousands of pests which seek out birds is one in particular which *you* may more closely encounter. Called the northern mite, you will know it is present in your bird room when you are subjected to an itching, especially on your hands and head, every time you linger with your birds. The itching can be intense, but you will survive. This arachnid is so small it will probably remain unseen, but it will take its toll, especially of birds which are very old, those which are very young, and those which have been sick. It sucks blood they can ill afford to lose, and it deprives them of sleep because they are preoccupied much of the time with itching.

You can control (and, with luck, eliminate) the northern mite with sprays and dusts available from pet shops and bird dealers. Just remember to remove all food and water before you spray. Get into cracks, nests, perch cracks—anywhere these little things could possibly creep. When they have fed, they are red or brown; when they are hungry they are gray. Always they are so small you may never see them—but by their itch you shall know them. Incidentally, these mites—and in fact *all* mites, lice, and ticks—are wingless.

REMEMBER: Some sprays and dusts may be used in limited quantities directly on birds, and others should be used only on the cages and aviary hardware, but *no insecticide should ever be permitted on water or food* (or even on cuttlebone).

This homemade wooden nest box (*left*) was designed with Gouldians in mind, as they prefer a dark, covered nest which offers privacy. A dowel perch has been fastened to the front of the nest box so that the parents can gain easy entry. *Below:* Mated pairs usually go to nest willingly.

Breeding Gouldians

BEHAVIOR

Whether you have one bird or a hundred, there will be active periods and quiet periods. Of course, all finches remain quiet during the dark hours, but during daylight hours a Gouldian is not constantly "on the go." You may witness ten or fifteen minutes of bathing followed by an equal period of drying and preening. Later there might be a ten-minute mealtime and a twenty-minute snooze, then another meal or nest making or a sunning-and-preening interlude, and so on through the day. It is perfectly normal for any healthy finch to snooze at midday for a half hour.

Obviously, a bird with its head tucked back between its wings *all day* is sick and needs isolation, warmth, antibiotics, and professional help. But with only a little luck, not too much work, and with patient application of your own powers of observation and intelligence, you will probably be able to maintain your birds for years with no problems or disease any worse than the need to clip their

claws—if and when they need it.

Young Gouldians will sit on perches and wait to be fed. Adult birds will also perch on twigs or dowels. An adult that sits on the floor is probably sick or about to die. At night young and adults frequently roost in their nests or in roosting nests which they build especially for nighttime use. An adult male may guide the young birds to the nest of their birth or to a roosting nest nightly for several weeks.

Why do young babies leave their nest? I speculate like this: It is nature's way that the nest cavity will fill up as the young birds develop. Parents will naturally continue to add grass, the young will naturally defecate around the rim, and, after the first few days, this material will not be removed. And, of course, the babies will naturally continue to grow. Each baby will be about ten times the volume of the egg it hatched from within fifteen days. All this naturally tends to *force* the youngsters out of their nest. They cannot remain, simply because there isn't enough room. This pressure to speed things up is, I continue to speculate, a function of the Australian climate. The rains stimulate plant growth, and the birds capitalize on the available short-term food supply; but they must work fast because the rainy season will not continue for very long and the urge to reproduce is very strong.

THE BREEDING CYCLE

This is rightly the subject of another book, but if you have a pair and conditions are right, your birds will surely try to reproduce themselves.

Isolate a pair that have been copulating, nest building, searching nest boxes, chasing other birds, or otherwise sending you a message. Give them one or, better still, two nest boxes. Buy or build boxes like the ones shown in the pictures.

The eggs are relatively large and snow-white. Leave them strictly alone. About four eggs are laid, but there may be as many as eight, one per day; serious incubation begins about the time all the eggs have been laid. Both parents take turns to incubate the eggs; however, the female invariably sits at night. Sometimes both birds incubate together, especially just before hatching time.

• Incubation takes about fourteen or fifteen days.

- Brooding continues, depending on temperature, for up to two weeks.
- By the second day after hatching, the young can be heard squeaking.
- Eyes open on or soon after the seventh day.
- Quills begin to show on the wings by the eleventh day.
- On or soon after the twenty-fifth day, the young leave the nest but will return to it at night, especially if the temperature drops.

Your caged birds should be checked daily when they are nesting, or not at all. If you plan to use seamless bands on the babies, the banding should not be your only visit; it may lead to desertion of the nest. If however, you look into every nest every day, your presence and smell will be part of the birds' environment, and the risk of nest desertion will be minimized. Be reconciled that you will lose a bird now and then. Young breeders frequently desert their first nest and then go on to years and years of successful production.

Your interference should be *constructive:*
- Provide each pair of birds with at least two nest boxes or baskets.
- Provide plenty of nesting material, dry grass stems, soft grass clippings, and feathers or wool or cotton scraps.
- Provide plenty of clean water for bathing; most birds must keep their eggs damp to ensure easy pipping at hatching time.
- Provide ample fresh food, green vegetables, hard-boiled eggs, cuttlebone, mineral supplements, sprouted seeds, dry seeds. Offer the supplements, but never neglect the basic diet ingredient, millet.
- Provide perches where it is warm and dry and draft-free.
- Provide quarters that are vermin-free.
- Provide a night light.
- Provide peace and quiet every night, all night.

By now you know whether you are going to remain as a passive bird keeper or are going to take that great leap forward into aviculture and become a serious breeder. This big step will cost some real money, and it will demand some real, time-consuming effort. If you elect to proceed, the rewards in satisfaction are tremendous, but (you had better believe) you still will never get rich by breeding Gouldian Finches (or by writing about them). Don't even try.

Remember, please, the chapters that follow are unnecessary for casual bird keepers; they are placed here to get you started only if you wish to propagate Gouldians.

In the natural order of things, there are never two species with absolutely identical diets, habits, defenses, and behavior which occupy the same niche. One and only one species will prevail. Other similar forms necessarily will be driven away or driven to extinction. If you don't believe me, ask Charles Darwin. What this means to a fancier of cage birds is that even among the various species of seedeating Australian finches *there are differences*. Gouldians and Zebras both come from Australia, both eat seeds, both are finches, but in nature and also in the cage or aviary they differ enough so that under some conditions Gouldians will die while Zebras breed like flies. There are subtle differences between these birds in habits and habitat. For you to succeed, you should not try to remake the bird, but rather you should try to create an artificial environment which mirrors what the particular species *wants to be accustomed to*.

TERRITORIES

Let's now look at the Gouldian as a bird which (unlike a House Sparrow, pigeon, or a gull) has carved only a very tiny niche in our globe to call its own. Put a pair of Gouldians in a breeding cage of, say, six cubic feet and they will be happy. Now put three pairs in three times as large a cage and there will be constant fighting for territories. I even went so far as to put three breeding pairs into a six-hundred-cubic-foot aviary, and still they were unable to get along amicably by either sharing or dividing the space. Each pair wanted all of it. Bear in mind that five or six cubic feet is adequate for one isolated pair to live and rear their young. But if you give them more, they want all of it.

When Gouldians squabble, they don't shed blood or even lose feathers, but there is certainly no shortage of fluttering and noisy chirping. Whether this strengthens the pair bonds or reduces the capacity to reproduce successfully, I don't know. There is no dearth of expert opinion on this subject, but without hard, scientific evidence I have yet to be convinced either way.

There is no doubt in my mind, however, that a cage or

aviary crowded with Society or Zebra finches, for example, is no place to breed Gouldians. What a pair of Gouldians will not do in a large aviary with fifty Zebras present is to breed as regularly and successfully as they will do with only one pair of Zebras—or better still, with none of these pests nearby. I call Zebras in a Gouldian breeding establishment pests reservedly, since they are useful for fostering, nearly as useful as Societies. These two species are also useful to "settle" shy, "wild" Gouldians.

Sometimes a Gouldian Finch will not bathe or eat hard-boiled egg or otherwise go along with "what it says in the book." Here is a situation where the commoner and bolder birds can help. Finches will learn more readily from other finches then they will from you. When Gouldians are caged with Zebras, they are prone to quickly adapt Zebra habits of bold inquisitiveness, vigorous and frequent bathing, and an appetite for a wide variety of foods. So use these birds to help, but don't keep them if crowding becomes a factor. I know that I mentioned this in a previous chapter; it bears repeating.

AGE FOR BREEDING

There are two distinct schools of thought about the age at which Gouldian Finches should be bred. One school holds that the birds should be the ones to decide when they are ready to breed and they then will do so when they are sexually mature. Temperature, length of daylight, and diet, of course, all have a profound effect, and it is entirely possible that under this system, young birds only a few months out of their own shells will breed and raise families. It is exactly for this reason that many other experienced breeders make sure that the birds are not provided with nesting materials and nest boxes until they are between eight and twelve months old; these people believe that letting the birds breed before that age is a mistake. Some authorities tell us that young females are prone to suffer from egg binding. I suspect that egg binding is more likely a result of poor nutrition and cold housing than a result of mating young birds. I have had juveniles breed successfully before their molt was completed. Whether this is a good practice for the long run remains to be seen. The weight of informed opinion is against this way of doing things.

BREEDING STOCK

You may want to control your breeding operation by caging individual pairs or small groups of pairs. You may keep an aviary with just one color variety and cull out all those that don't match. You may opt for letting nature take its course and provide no control whatsoever over an aviary full of birds. The choice is up to you. The more you control, the better you can predict the outcome of your breeding goals—but you must work much harder: more cages to clean, babies to band, records to keep.

My only advice is to start with robust birds and act promptly and ruthlessly to keep the quality up. Inbreeding of defective birds is a game for fools. As to the breeding stock you start with: be selective. Don't fall in love with the first one-eyed, half-feathered, wry-tailed bird you see. Shop around, pay a fair price, and then breed up, not down.

Any color Gouldian Finch will mate with any other Gouldian Finch of the opposite sex. Any Gouldian Finch old enough to show its colors is old enough to reproduce itself, but many experienced breeders of show-quality birds will not permit breeding with any specimen younger than eight months. And remember, any Gouldian Finch may desert its first nest and then go on to be an excellent producer for the next few years.

NESTS

Most wild Gouldian Finch nests are located in holes. Some northern-hemisphere birds with somewhat similar nesting habits which you may already be familiar with are the American Bluebird and the European Starling. These species also sometimes nest in abandoned nests of other birds, hollow trees, fence-post knotholes, and man-made boxlike structures.

One account of Australian Gouldian nests mentions a hole in a termite nest. This could put it easily six feet or so above the surrounding ground level and close to a source of food, since wild Gouldians are known to eat flying termites, especially during the Gouldian breeding season.

The nests are rarely built "from scratch" in the open, so you should not expect your birds to do it that way in captivity. Provide boxes, jug-shaped large baskets, and, if you keep your birds in an aviary, try hollow sections of log—an old apple tree usually has several such. (If there is such a thing as an old apple tree anymore—most people nowadays prune off dead limbs and plug up the hollow ones.)

The nest cup may be constructed of relatively coarse grass. It will not be lined with feathers. In fact, it might not even be grassed, but the four-to-seven pure white eggs will be deposited right on the soft punky wood often found in a tree-trunk hole.

If you provide several optional nest sites in an aviary, the chances are good that the birds will choose the one which has its opening facing the light. Perhaps the adults need this light to find the babies in order to feed them.

Gouldians are known to copulate in the nest rather than in the open. Obviously, this could never happen in one of those tiny basket nests which are so popular for Zebra Finches.

Remember that a Gouldian is not a creeper like a woodpecker or a nuthatch. I forgot this just once when I provided a hollow log for a nest site. I fastened it securely to a large base so it would stand straight and put a handful of punky wood in the base. The opening was thirty inches off the floor. The male was attracted, and he enticed a female to enter. She went to the bottom, was trapped, and died of exhaustion after a few hours. The same log on its side later made a great nest site.

All this suggests that these finches naturally lay in covered nests. More evidence that the nest interiors are naturally dark is that newly hatched Gouldian Finches have luminous (perhaps we could call it phosphorescent) marks at the corners of the mouths, which are believed to facilitate the delivery of food in a darkened nest.

If conditions are good enough, your female birds will put their eggs on the cage floor—you cannot stop the egg-laying process. If conditions are wrong, no nest-box design will induce a female to lay any eggs at all.

Boxes vs. baskets—both work, but boxes with easily removable covers will be better for you if you plan to swap eggs, foster, band, or otherwise manipulate your birds. A covered basket is great if you plan to let nature take its course. Whether you build or buy the nests depends on your skills. A well-built box or basket is inexpensive and may be reused for years. Remember to get or build a box design which you can open for examination and for cleaning.

Two clutches of eggs in a Gouldian nest. As many as eight eggs can be incubated in one nest with success, but a normal clutch is more nearly four.

Provide punky wood in the nest bottom or soft grass in the cage, and the birds may build or shape a cavity. Some do a little weaving and some don't. I would not advise using sawdust from green wood but rather something old, punky, soft, and almost peaty. The nest material ought not be bone dry. If it is, the adult birds will probably moisten it by bathing and then sitting in the nest as they dry out. A bone-dry egg on a bone-dry nest under a bone-dry incubating bird will probably die in the shell.

Here is a true story. It happened while I was photographing some of the birds which appear in this book. In the beginning I hung several nest boxes and baskets in an aviary so that the birds could choose freely. I half-filled one box with soft grass. A pair of young Gouldians threw all the grass out of the box until they were down to the bare wood. Not one shred or leaf or stem remained. Then the hen laid two eggs, a day apart, right on that bare wood. I didn't believe it. So, to help Mother Nature, I spooned up the eggs and put some punky wood under them. On the third day there was a third egg; on the fourth day the nest box was half-stuffed with soft grass—on top of the punky wood—and a fourth egg had been laid. Incubation commenced with a fifth egg, on the sixth day. From then on I'm happy to relate the birds followed the procedures as they are set forth in the books that people write about Gouldian Finches.

Remember that wild Gouldian Finches are reported to be opportunistic nesters. The domestic strains we are working with cannot be expected to follow more rigid patterns of behavior. Furthermore, they can't read. Give your birds plenty of room, food, water, minerals, warmth, humidity, privacy, security, and nesting facilities and materials—they will almost surely take care of propagating their species (even if we aren't too sure of their *modus operandi* or of their genus).

But my true story isn't finished yet. The nest box I referred to didn't admit enough light to permit photography, so I built another nest box, larger, with a hinged front door and a chimney-like opening on top to accommodate a small photoflash unit. Then I swapped the nest boxes. That is, I chased the hen off her eggs and removed the sloppy grass pad and the punky wood from the original box and put this material with the clutch of eggs into the new box. Within five minutes the bird was back sitting on her eggs. I am not certain that all domestic Gouldians are this easy to manipulate and manage, but if so, then fostering with Societies or Zebras is unneccessary except for "factory" production. One could almost use Gouldians to foster the really difficult finch species.

EGGS

Gouldian Finch eggs are white, slightly glossy, and the minor diameter is not always midway between the ends. This can also be said of Zebra and Society finch eggs, but eggs of these two species tend to be a trifle smaller.

A few eggs sampled at random in my aviary measured as follows:

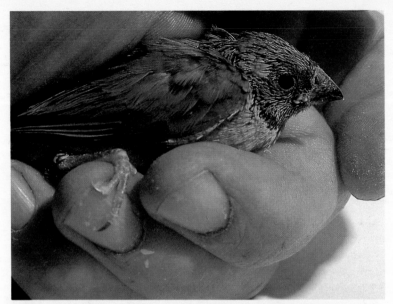

The luminous blue mouth markings (tubercules) at the base of the bill are still evident on this youngster (*above*). The same bird (*below*) several days later. A careful breeder would know from his records that this bird is a Red-head, even though its juvenile plumage gives no indication of this.

Gouldians will build their nests in side-mounted baskets, although generally they prefer nest boxes or hollow logs.

	Society	Gouldian	Zebra
Major diameter	.585	.675	.560
in inches	.566	.647	.555
Minor diameter	.435	.475	.440
in inches	.424	.472	.441

The reason for this egg description, in view of the fact that it is beyond your control, is that if you have these three species together in an aviary or a large breeding cage, a nest might well contain eggs from all three. Although Society and Zebra eggs are incubated for about two weeks and Gouldians might require up to several additional days, it is possible to raise all three in one nest. As I mentioned before, these three species lay white eggs, and white eggs usually come from birds that nest in dark places.

Incubation begins on the day or the day after the last egg is laid, and it continues for about fifteen days. The female seems to put in more hours on the nest than the male. She generally sits out the night, in addition to her daytime duties. Don't be shaken if you find both parents in the nest box at the same time. They may do that too, especially during the last few days of incubation.

If, just prior to hatching time, your birds show a special interest in taking baths, it may be that they sense dry eggs and this is their way of correcting the problem. Good!—let them bathe to their heart's content.

The eggs will open up from the inside, which is to say they need no help, just parental warmth and perhaps that extra moisture. Hatching birds are naturally furnished with a tiny, sharp "tooth" on the tip of the upper beak which cuts through the membrane and shell. The blind, naked chick actually chips a ring around the shell, which then pops open. The adult birds remove the empty shell halves from the nest. They will eat the shells—at least this is what usually happens.

As an afterthought, I might mention that you should expect an 80% success ratio from your eggs. Over the long haul, eight of every ten eggs should hatch. If they don't, you should cage separate pairs and stop all that social interplay until you find the culprit or the other reasons for your lack of success.

If you find that fertile eggs are not hatching and you have no clue as to the trouble, try misting the nest with a fine spray of water at a temperature of about 95 F. The water may aid the chick to chip through its shell. That temperature is suggested so that you don't chill it to death while you are helping it to live. Commence spraying, or let's call it misting, on the twelfth day of incubation and continue on a once-daily basis until you get a decent hatch or until all hope is gone. If your birds bathe frequently and the humidity is high, this misting might not be necessary, but if all else fails and you are sure the eggs are fertile, it is certainly worth a try.

INCUBATION

The female lays the eggs, then she and her mate sit on them, and within fifteen days they hatch. Simple and sometimes true, but far from the whole truth; the exceptions are the challenges of aviculture. Let's try again with a little more detail.

While the nest is being built, the female deposits one white egg. It may have a creamy pink cast to it; this is not shell color, but it is just the color of the yolk transmitted through the thin shell. During the course of the week that the rest of the eggs are being laid, the male will continue to deliver nest material, and the female will weave it into a sloppy, covered tunnel. Sometimes they don't build a nest, rather they appropriate the nest of another bird or simply deposit their eggs on the bottom of a hollow tree on punky wood.

Even before that first egg was deposited, one or both birds will have been sitting in the nest. That is to say, the eggless nest might have been occupied by one or sometimes (especially at night) two birds. This is quite a tight situation. I recommend a square-bottomed box with a minimum dimension of four inches.

THE YOUNG

By the third day, the chicks cry faintly for food. By the end of a week, they make a racket that can be heard anywhere in your bird room. Both parents feed the young on the same food they have been eating. You should pro-

Finch nest baskets (*above*) are available in most pet shops.
Several generations of Gouldians were fledged successfully from
this model. The youngster below is still a nestling, content to
nestle in a hand.

Society Finches have proven to be reliable foster parents for Gouldian eggs and chicks as well as for other finch species.

vide soaked and sprouted seeds, half-ripe grass seeds from a lawn, and additional hard-boiled egg. The adults will swallow hulled seeds and soft plant leaves and regurgitate them into the gullets of the babies. The youngsters' eyes open on the tenth day, plus or minus two days. A four-week-old bird will leave the nest during the day, but may return at night. Juveniles have dark grey or blackish bills which gradually take on the adult colors as they molt.

Under ideal conditions, breeding cycles may overlap. When this happens, the female will stay with her new eggs and the male will feed the previous nestful of birds. Adults in their fourth year will still rear large clutches of healthy, robust young. Obviously some birds are better at it than others. I suspect that birds which were fostered don't make the best parents. Some breeders make a big thing about separating the sexes to limit production. This is a subject that many experts argue about.

WAIFS

Sometimes a baby bird will be pushed out of the nest by its siblings or by the accident of clasping its parent when that bird takes wing. On other occasions, one or both parents desert the nest or are lost. Well, regardless of the cause, all is not lost if you have another nest of Gouldians or Society Finches or Zebras at the same stage of development. The options are nearly unlimited. You can swap fledglings which are in trouble with a good chance that their survival rate will improve as a result of your manipulations. If the risk of death is imminent, obviously any action you take is better than no action at all.

Dehydration and cold are two big problems you must overcome. Okay, you pick up a pinfeathered waif—say, ten days old—from the cage or aviary floor. Its crop is empty, and it is cold. You don't know which nest it came from; there are several with same-sized nestlings in the area. First, hold the bird in your cupped hand and blow air over it from your mouth. This air is warm, over 95 F. It is moist. It contains carbon dioxide, which stimulates respiration in animals. Hopefully this treatment will rejuvenate the bird within twenty minutes or less. Next, get a little sweetened water into its crop. A few drops down its throat from a clean insulin syringe will suffice. You may also want to feed the bird if your manual dexterity is good. This can be accomplished by dampening a broomstraw in water and picking up some hulled seeds on the end of the straw. These may be rubbed off into the squeaker's mouth as you hold the bird in your hand. Remember that tens of thousands of parrots and parrotlike birds have been hand-raised—this is nothing new. The only problem is size. Finches start out very, very small.

After providing warmth and a drink and perhaps a meal, you should choose the nest in which to place the young bird. I don't recommend an incubator and a brooder and a routine of hand-feeding for raising every Gouldian waif. Just get it back on its feet and then promptly relocate it with others of the same or slightly younger age. This will give the waif an advantage. Don't end up with more than eight babies in a nest—this would overly burden the parents.

FOSTERING

In aviculture, fostering is usually accomplished by putting the eggs of a "difficult" bird into the nest of a similar but "easy" species. The Whooping Crane has been fostered by the Sandhill Crane. Bantam chickens (famous for being broody and tolerant) will foster quail, pheasants, other varieties of chicken, and will even brood golf balls.

One reason for fostering is that a female bird will often lay another clutch of eggs if the first clutch was removed. A rare bird might be induced to lay two or even three times as many eggs as it would normally in its breeding season. Another reason for resorting to fostering is that some domestic birds make poor parents, so we choose better parents to incubate the eggs and raise the babies. Several varieties of pigeon, for example, have such short bills that it is difficult for them to feed their own babies, so pigeon keepers resort to fostering to propagate them.

Gouldian Finches have been fostered for years, especially in Japan, in order to maximize productivity—purely a commercial reason. Under normal conditions in non-commercial aviaries this fostering is not done because the Gouldian is a really good parent and a prolific breeder. Yes, Gouldians are relatively delicate, but if you give them wholesome food and the required environment, they will

A nest of four youngsters. Their eyes open around the tenth day, and their dark bills lighten as they mature. The wing feathers are not yet fully developed, but enclosed in feather sheaths.

Facing page, above: It is reasonable to expect a Gouldian to molt its feathers at intervals throughout its life. The white specks on the head of this Red-headed male are feather sheaths which have not yet opened. *Below:* An open plastic band helps breeders keep track of their pairs in an aviary.

have no trouble bringing up their own babies. You should get about a dozen young from each pair of breeders every year, without resorting to fostering.

If you want to try fostering, I can think of no legal or moral or economic reason why you should not. The only reason for not fostering which I have ever heard and which makes some sense is that a baby Gouldian which was fostered might not know it was a Gouldian and might not be a good parent. Evidence?—I have no evidence.

The best foster for a Gouldian is a Society Finch. Zebra Finches will also foster Gouldians. Societies go to work especially well in cages (better in cages than Zebras) and so for fostering they are favored. With "factory" fostering you might get as many as three dozen salable birds from a pair of breeders every year.

If you keep several pairs of Societies for each pair of Gouldians, you can, with a little juggling, always have a pair of Societies which will go to nest about the same time as the Gouldians. The more caged pairs you have, the better your chances for perfect timing. Fortunately the timing need not be absolutely perfect. Two or three days between the first-egg dates is okay. All you need is a small plastic spoon, a little dexterity, and some thoughtful manipulation. The birds will take care of the rest.

A few things you should bear in mind, in no particular order:

• Birds cannot count. You can remove a clutch of Society eggs and replace it with one or two more or fewer Gouldian eggs, and no bird will be the wiser.

• The oils and odors in your skin might discourage the foster parents or kill the embryos in their shells. Don't finger the eggs, but rather handle them with a small metal or plastic spoon.

• There is no need in this process for an incubator.

• There is no need to mark the eggs.

• There is a need to have easily accessible nest boxes. Many baskets are shaped so it would be impossible to spoon out the eggs without risk of breakage, so use boxes with doors.

• There is no need for fear and trepidation—fostering of Gouldians by Societies and Zebras is really not difficult if you are determined to try.

• Make the move in one operation. Don't bother with one egg at a time, but rather take all the Gouldian eggs as soon as you believe the clutch is complete. Gouldian eggs take a day or two longer to hatch than do Societies' or Zebras', but if the eggs are fertile, the foster parents will stick it out with no problems for you.

• This is the time when warmth, humidity, freedom from drafts, good nutrition, and rest are most critical.

• Your birds are prolific—you can get a female to lay clutches of five eggs as frequently as every month; you can foster these eggs under Societies and Zebras; you can crowd the babies into small cages—and you can also watch your whole house of cards fall down. You have already paid for this advice; hopefully you will take it. In the beginning, at least, don't try to get rich in the Gouldian-factory business. It just won't work.

RULE BREAKERS

When we deal with domesticated cage birds, or for that matter with any living creature, two things invariably happen. First: we make and record observations. For many people the record then becomes the rule. Second: we discover as we read the records of observations by other people that all the individuals don't always do it the same way.

For example, on p. 40 of *American Cage-Bird Magazine,* Jan. 1980, in a letter to the editor, a lady who is both a medical doctor and also a doctor of philosophy writes about her pair of breeding Gouldians. These birds have raised two broods per year for over the previous two summers for a total of 12 babies, in a living-room flight cage. The cage is 5 ½ x 2 x 3 ft., and in it are the one pair of Gouldians, a pair of breeding cordonblues, one Society Finch and two other pairs of waxbills. The room is a living room with a TV and a stereo; it is used for entertaining.

These birds eat the usual seeds (canary, rape, and millet) with supplements including Petamine, shredded carrots, apple slices, and dandelion greens. The doctor then goes on to tell us that "when the eggs hatch, I give mealworms, about five per day." What prompted those Gouldians to eat mealworms is an interesting question. Perhaps they learned from the waxbills or the cordonbleus. Regardless, it was a good lesson they learned, even

An open plastic band (*above*) is easy to remove and replace. The Red-headed female (*facing page*) wears a colored, numbered band. The banding of birds is a convenient way of identifying and selecting breeding pairs when several Gouldians are housed together.

if *as a general rule* caged Gouldians eat only vegetable matter and perhaps hard-boiled egg.

BANDING

If you are serious about breeding more than one pair of Gouldian Finches, you should keep track of your birds with bands. There are two basic types of bands. The first type band is the permanent, or closed, band which is a seamless ring, usually made of aluminum, anodized, and available in many permanent colors. Seamless bands are inexpensive even when they are custom-made with your initials and some system of numbering stamped into the metal. The closed band remains on the bird for its lifetime. You will slip it on a nestling when it is between four and seven days old—certainly before it is twelve days old—sliding it over the three forward toes, past the pad of the foot, then up the lower leg until it clears the rear toe. You may need a broomstraw to help get the band past the rear toe. A little petroleum jelly will help. The ring then slips down on the leg and remains loose but permanently in place for the life of the bird.

Breeders will order bands in a different color every year so that the age of the bird will be apparent even without close examination. Of course, the number of the band should be recorded in a ledger, along with other numbers of that clutch and of the parent birds.

An alternate to the closed band is the kind that has some sort of seam somewhere. It may be a springy plastic ring, and it usually bears a number or a letter. Of course, these too are available in various colors. Seamed, or open, bands are often used by breeders just to keep track of pairs or sexes. Combinations of colors on the left or right or both feet will provide the information at a glance. These may be removed at the end of a breeding season.

Another type of band made of plastic is simply a colored spring-coil which bears no number. This too is useful in an aviary where many pairs might otherwise not be sortable. Still another version of open band is often used by banders of wild birds; it is a numbered metal band which is closed loosely around the adult bird's leg with a pliers-type tool. Pet shops that specialize in small birds can get these bands for you or lead you to a source of them. Look for advertisements in avicultural magazines or ask members of the bird-breeders' club which you might want to join. Bands are inexpensive and readily available; don't try to make your own.

The first time you try to band a fledgling, you will surely wonder if you dare. But bear in mind that over the centuries many people, far clumsier, managed with patience and gentle firmness; you will also. One suggestion: sit down at a desk or table to do the job, at least for the first time. If you are off your feet, your hands will be steadier. If you can brace your arms or elbows on a smooth, level surface, you will be steadier still. A second suggestion: don't permit anyone who hasn't already banded a baby bird to be in the same room with you the first time you band one. It really is not that difficult, and with these suggestions it will be still easier. When your permanently banded bird wins a prize, any doubts about the justification for banding will vanish, absolutely.

If you band your birds and keep accurate records, you are ready to apply the principles of genetics to your breeding program, so let's consider that subject next.

The specimen at the left, a mature male, is molting his head feathers. The healthy young Red-headed female below is in a partial head molt.

Gouldian Genetics

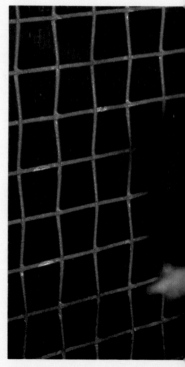

There is but one species of Gouldian Finch. As I mentioned elsewhere, its generic name is still in limbo, but all over the world the common name—Gouldian Finch—means the same bird to everyone. All wild and domestic Gouldians are part of the same population, the same genetic pool. Modern classifiers are generally agreed that the one species (whatever its scientific name might be) is not split into various subspecies or races. This may be confusing at first glance, since we all know that there are red-headed, black-headed, yellow-headed, white-breasted, lutino, pied, and albino forms. Liken these to the color variations found in cats or dogs or domestic pigeons and go on from there. A yellow- or liver-colored or black Labrador retriever is not a subspecies of dog or even a race apart; it too is simply a variety of a species.

Any color of Gouldian Finch may be mated to any other of the opposite sex—all the color combinations will produce fertile and healthy young—and when these young

mature, they will take on colors which you should be able to predict by applying genetic principles. Stop!—this is too easy. Nothing in nature is so simple. Let's take a moment to learn a few special words, then on to Gregor Mendel!

Dominant. A genetic trait which requires but one gene of a pair to make itself evident.
Recessive. A genetic trait which does not become evident unless two matched genes are aligned.
Homozygous. Pure for a particular genetic trait—matched genes.
Heterozygous. Split; the pair of genes are not the same—unmatched. The dominant gene gives the organism its outward appearance.
Split. Heterozygous, or hybrid, for a particular genetic trait. A normal-colored bird with a recessive gene for albino is said to be "normal split for albino."
Hybrid. Split
Pure. Homozygous. May be dominant *or* recessive.
Mendel's Laws. The basis of the science of heredity developed by an Austrian monk-botanist, Gregor J. Mendel (1822–84).

As you get started, you must fully understand several things. The first is that a genetic trait is usually predictable, but the prediction is often stated as a statistical probability. One good example is your own sex. There is in humans an even chance that every baby will be either male or female. Call it 50% and be grateful. This "flip of the coin" takes place every time there is a conception. The odds each time are 50-50. You may be one of five children, all the same sex. That doesn't in any way influence the sex of your next sibling. The odds each time are still 50-50. As an aside, I might mention that armadillos produce young which for any litter are all the same sex. You may liken this armadillo phenomenon to identical human multiple births.

The second point that needs clarification is that some colors of birds are affected by environmental or nutritional factors. Temperature, humidity, and light duration and intensity are all known to affect feather color. With

A Black-headed Gouldian adult. Although the Red-headed factor is dominant over the Black-headed factor, Black-heads outnumber Red-heads three-to-one in the wild.

A young Red-headed female.

The intensity of color in the Red-headed male coming in for a landing contrasts with the subdued tones of the female's plumage (*facing page*).

Zebra Finches, for example, certain vitamins are linked to the degree of blackness. By changing any of these environmental factors, colors are altered, but the process (in these instances) is reversible. Modify the hours of daylight or the diet, and the color will change again with the next molt. With these two minor points established, we can proceed to look at the birds as they are found in Australia.

The two more common forms of Gouldians are the black-headed and the red-headed. Let's start with them. To begin with, the ratio in the wild is three black-headed to one red-headed. The lines are poorly drawn, as some red-heads are brighter than others, but that is the way Mother Nature works.

In 1946 in the *Avicultural Magazine,* H. N. Southern laid out the basics for Gouldian genetics, and it has been confirmed and amplified many times since then. Simply stated, red-heads are *sex-linked* and *dominant* over black-heads. A chart will help. It might not make much sense at first glance, but your effort in understanding now will pay off later.

Sex linkage means that the genetic trait we are considering is located on the very same chromosome that also determines the sex of the bird. Among birds it takes two X sex chromosomes to make a male. Thus XX represents a male when we consider sex-linked traits. But a female bird is female because it has but one X-chromosome, and this X-chromosome is linked in every cell to a Y-chromosome; so to abbreviate, XY represents a female.

When any male (XX) and any female (XY) are mated we diagram their union thus:

	X	Y ← Female
Male → X	XX	XY
X	XX	XY

This tells us graphically what we already know: namely, 50% of the offspring will be female (XY) and the remainder will be male (XX). There is no guarantee that every clutch of eggs will be exactly 50-50, but over the very long haul that is the way it is.

Now when a color trait is sex-linked (on the

X-chromosome) and it is dominant, any bird with just one such chromosome will exhibit that color. Let's look at that diagram again, but this time let's add an R to the X-chromosome to show dominant red-headedness. A female with a red head $(X^R Y)$ is mated to a black-headed male (XX):

	X^R	Y
X	$X^R X$	XY
X	$X^R X$	XY

Fifty percent of a large population would be red-headed heterozygous males $(X^R X)$ and 50% would be black-headed females (XY). All the male progeny will be red-headed $(X^R X)$ since the needed single gene for dominant red-headedness is present. The diagram also shows that all the females (XY) from this union will be black-headed.

A male Gouldian Finch could be red-headed because one X-chromosome carries the R for red-headedness, or because the other one does, or because both do. $X^R X$ or XX^R is a red-headed male. Out of convention we would write both of them as $X^R X$. Birds like these are also known as single-factor, or split, or heterozygous, for this dominant color trait. $X^R X^R$ is also a red-headed male. This bird would be called double-factor, or pure, or homozygous, for this genetically controlled color trait. Since in this case red is dominant, we conventionally write a capital (R) for it and would use a lower-case letter (r) for black-headedness. (I omitted this symbol to keep the diagrams simple as you get started.)

Now, the red-headed trait is tied only to the X-chromosome, and all female Gouldian Finches are designated XY. If a female is a red-head it must be because her one X-chromosome carries the dominant (R) gene. So, she is shown in our diagrams as $X^R Y$. There cannot be an R superscript on the Y-chromosome.

Now let's look at another diagram. Here's a split red-headed male $(X^R X)$ mated to a black-headed female (XY):

The Blue-breast (*above*), found only in captivity, is recessive to the purple breast of the wild forms (*facing page*).

	X	Y
X^R	$X^R X$	$X^R Y$
X	XX	XY

Fifty percent of the male progeny will be red-headed ($X^R X$), and the remainder of the males will be black-headed (XX). Fifty percent of the female progeny will be red-headed ($X^R Y$), and the remainder of the females will be black-headed (XY).

The next chart is for a pure (homozygous) red-headed male ($X^R X^R$) mated to a black-headed female (XY):

	X	Y
X^R	$X^R X$	$X^R Y$
X^R	$X^R X$	$X^R Y$

Since in this example all the female progeny are red-headed, we know that the male was a double-factor—pure for red-headedness; he had to be. We also see from this diagram that all the males produced from this union will be red-headed.

So now you are becoming more familiar with the terms: single-factor vs. double-factor, split vs. pure, or heterozygous vs. homozygous.

When we look at any black-headed male we know he has no genetic material in his cells for red-headedness; but when we look at a red-headed male, we don't know if he is pure (homozygous, double-factored) for red-headedness or if he is just split (heterozygous, single-factored) red-headed. To find out, we must breed from him a large enough sample to demonstrate a high statistical probability. You could, for example, mate a red-headed male of unknown pedigree with a black-headed female. To have reasonable assurance that you have eliminated chance, you should have about a dozen young in your sample. If any black-headed offspring are produced, you can be certain that the male was split. Another thing you can be sure of is that if both parent birds are black-headed, all their progeny will be black-headed. Also, if both parents are red-headed but even one black-headed female is ever produced from such a union, then the male must have been split (single-factor, heterozygous) for red-headedness.

Finally, please bear in mind that all this information about red-headedness in Gouldians is tied to a sex-linked dominant trait. For a simple recessive color trait, read on. A yellow-headed Gouldian in the wild is a rare bird indeed. Immelmann tells us that in the wild they occur in the proportion of one yellow-head for every one thousand to five thousand of the black- or red-headed forms. Genetically this yellow-headedness is a recessive trait. It is not sex-linked. It must be present on both chromosomes before you can see it.

How does sex-linkage interact with yellow-headedness? How do the lutinos and albinos, white-breasted, and other new color varieties interact? These questions are beyond the scope of this book, and, in fact, at the time of this writing, there isn't too much we know with absolute certainty about these mutations. Much of what has been written on this subject is incomplete or inaccurate; be patient.

EXTENDING YOURSELF

I hope I have anticipated your problems with Gouldians and that now you can relax and enjoy them. Much of your fun and satisfaction and help will come from membership in an avicultural society. If you want to breed any species of finches, you should budget some time for joining a club, attending meetings, and participating in the shows.

Also, subscribe to a magazine if your society does not publish one of its own. To make a beginning, you should start with a copy of the *American Cage-Bird Magazine* (3449 N. Western Ave., Chicago, IL. 60618), which publishes a list of clubs in every issue. Write to the club or association secretary whose address or name looks best to you.

In the United States, other leading avicultural magazines you should sample are *The A.F.A. Watchbird* (published by the American Federation of Aviculture, Box 1568, Redondo Beach, CA 90278) and *Bird World* (Box 70, North Hollywood, CA 91603).

In Great Britain I suggest you sample *Cage and Aviary Birds* (Surrey House, 1 Throwley Way, Sutton, Surrey, England).